EXTREME SCIENCE EXPLORERS

EXPLORE THE SUN

Tricia Hoffman

Enslow PUBLISHING

Please visit our website, www.enslow.com. For a free color catalog of all our high-quality books, call toll free 1-800-398-2504 or fax 1-877-980-4454

Published in 2027 by
Enslow Publishing
2544 Clinton Street
Buffalo, NY 14224

Portions of this work were originally authored by Claire Flynn and published as *Fantastic Science Journeys: A Trip to the Sun*. All new material in this edition is authored by Tricia Hoffman.

Cataloging-in-Publication Data
Names: Hoffman, Tricia.
Title: Explore the sun / Tricia Hoffman.
Description: Buffalo, NY : Enslow Publishing, 2027. | Series: Extreme science explorers | Includes glossary and index.
Identifiers: ISBN 9781978549111 (pbk.) | ISBN 9781978549128 (library bound) | ISBN 9781978549135 (ebook)
Subjects: LCSH: Sun--Juvenile literature. | Solar energy--Juvenile literature.
Classification: LCC QB521.5 H644 2027 | DDC 523.7--dc23

Printed in China

Photos Credits: Cover, p. 1 IlmariP Photos/Shutterstock.com; p. 3 Gergitek/Shutterstock.com; p. 4 Mabeline72/Shutterstock.com; p. 4 Ekrem Canli/Wikimedia Austria; p. 6 sdecoret/Shutterstock.com; p. 8 Ezequiel Etcheverry/Shutterstock.com; p. 10 BankBever/Shutterstock.com; p. 11 Nazarii_Neshcherenskyi/Shutterstock.com; p. 12 Wikipedia/Wikipedia; p. 15 Zaporizhzhia vector/Shutterstock.com; p. 16 illstudio/Shutterstock.com; p. 17 Suzanne Tucker/Shutterstock.com; p. 18 NASA/NASA; p. 20 Abstract51/Shutterstock.com; p. 22 Withan Tor/Shutterstock.com; p. 23 Meletios Verras/Shutterstock.com; p. 24 Aleksandr Ozerov/Shutterstock.com; p. 25 Lifestyle Travel Photo/Shutterstock.com; p. 26 NASA/NASA; p. 28 Sergey Novikov/Shutterstock.com; p. 29 Wikipedia/Wikipedia; p. 31 Pike-28/Shutterstock.com

CPSIA compliance information: Batch #QSENS27: For further information, contact Enslow Publishing, New York, New York, at 1-800-398-2504.

TABLE OF CONTENTS

THE BRIGHT HOT SUN

Have you ever looked up at the sky and wanted to learn more about that huge, glowing ball? The sun is quite important! It is at the center of our solar system. Without it, life on Earth wouldn't exist!

Just like all stars, the sun is a glowing, spinning ball made of very hot gases. Earth and all of the other objects in our solar system **orbit** around it. This is because of **gravity**. The gravity holds our entire solar system together.

Let's take a closer look at the sun and what makes it so amazing!

THAT'S EXTREME!

Never look directly at the sun. You could hurt your eyes. ***Astronomers*** *use special telescopes that allow them to safely take a closer look.*

Without the warmth and light from the sun, Earth would be a cold and dark place.

The moon is much closer to Earth than the sun is.

THE CLOSEST STAR

The sun is the closest star to Earth. But it is still very far away! The sun is about 93 million miles (150 million km) from Earth. If we could hop into a car and drive to the sun at 70 miles (113 km) per hour, it would take us about 152 years to get there!

However, the distance is a good thing. The sun puts off so much heat that if we were too close, it would be way too hot! The sun is essential for life on Earth. It provides energy for plants to grow and therefore humans to exist!

THAT'S EXTREME!

It takes about eight minutes for the sun's light to reach Earth. This means that when you see the sun, you're actually seeing it as it looked eight minutes ago.

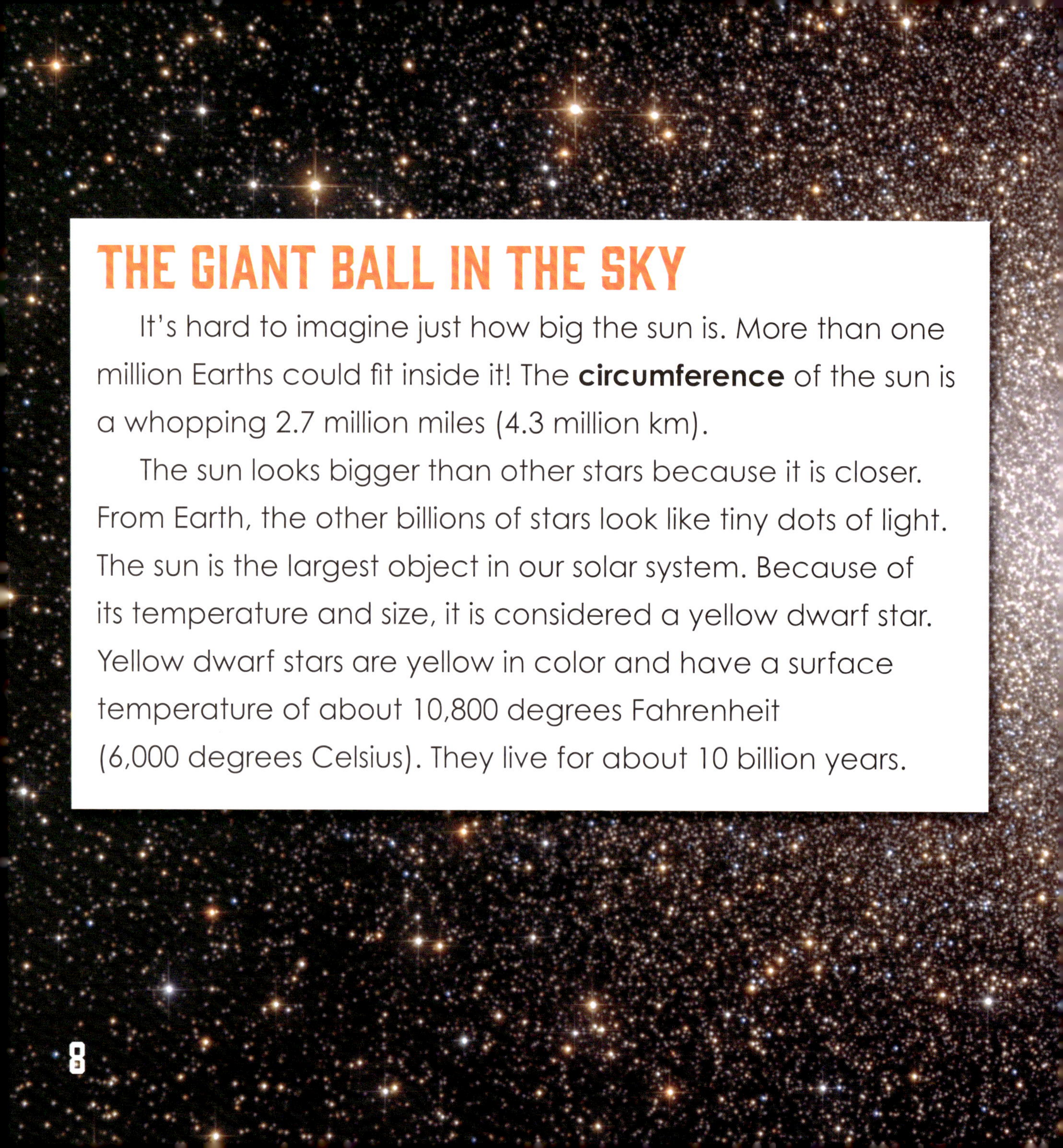

THE GIANT BALL IN THE SKY

It's hard to imagine just how big the sun is. More than one million Earths could fit inside it! The **circumference** of the sun is a whopping 2.7 million miles (4.3 million km).

The sun looks bigger than other stars because it is closer. From Earth, the other billions of stars look like tiny dots of light. The sun is the largest object in our solar system. Because of its temperature and size, it is considered a yellow dwarf star. Yellow dwarf stars are yellow in color and have a surface temperature of about 10,800 degrees Fahrenheit (6,000 degrees Celsius). They live for about 10 billion years.

There are more stars in the universe than there are grains of sand on Earth!

THAT'S EXTREME!

The sun is huge, but it's an average size for a star. Scientists have discovered stars that are much bigger, but also stars that are much smaller.

The sun is slowly getting brighter. When it was first created, it was a little dimmer than it is now.

GROWING IN SIZE

The sun started out as a large, puffy ball of gas. It was called a protostar. Billions of years ago, this cloud of gases and dust came together under the force of gravity. The pressure and heat increased, and the ball grew hotter and hotter. It became so hot that its core **ignited**, causing nuclear fusion.

Nuclear fusion is the process by which stars produce their own energy. Stars change hydrogen into helium and give off energy in the process.

Sometimes, the sun gives off a lot of energy. Other times, it gives off less energy. This pattern is called the solar cycle. The sun goes through one solar cycle about every 11 years.

THAT'S EXTREME!

The sun was created about 4.5 billion years ago. In another 5 billion years, the sun will become what's called a red giant.

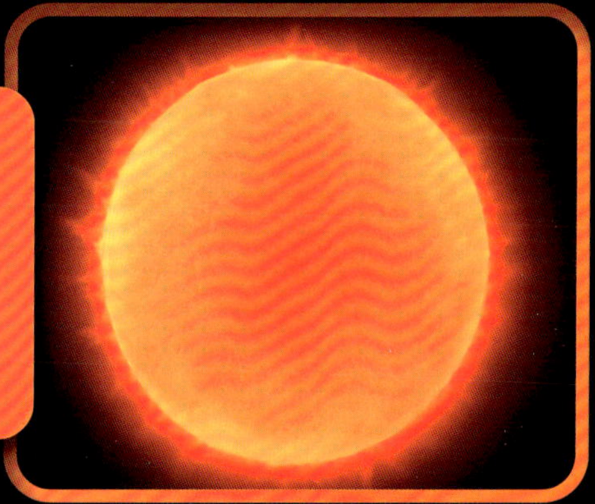

THE HOT, HOT SUN

The surface of the sun is about 10,000 degrees Fahrenheit (5,538 degrees Celsius)! If that's too hot for you, we'll look for some sunspots. Sunspots are parts of the sun that are cooler than other parts of the sun. They appear darker on images taken by astronomers.

Sunspots happen because the sun's magnetic fields get twisted and tangled. Some spots get cooler, so they look darker. But these spots aren't permanent. They don't always exist in the same place. Even the number of sunspots on our sun can change. Astronomers use special telescopes that allow them to see these sunspots.

THAT'S EXTREME!

If we were to reach the sun's core, it would get even hotter. The core reaches more than 27,000,000 degrees Fahrenheit (115,000,000 degrees Celsius)!

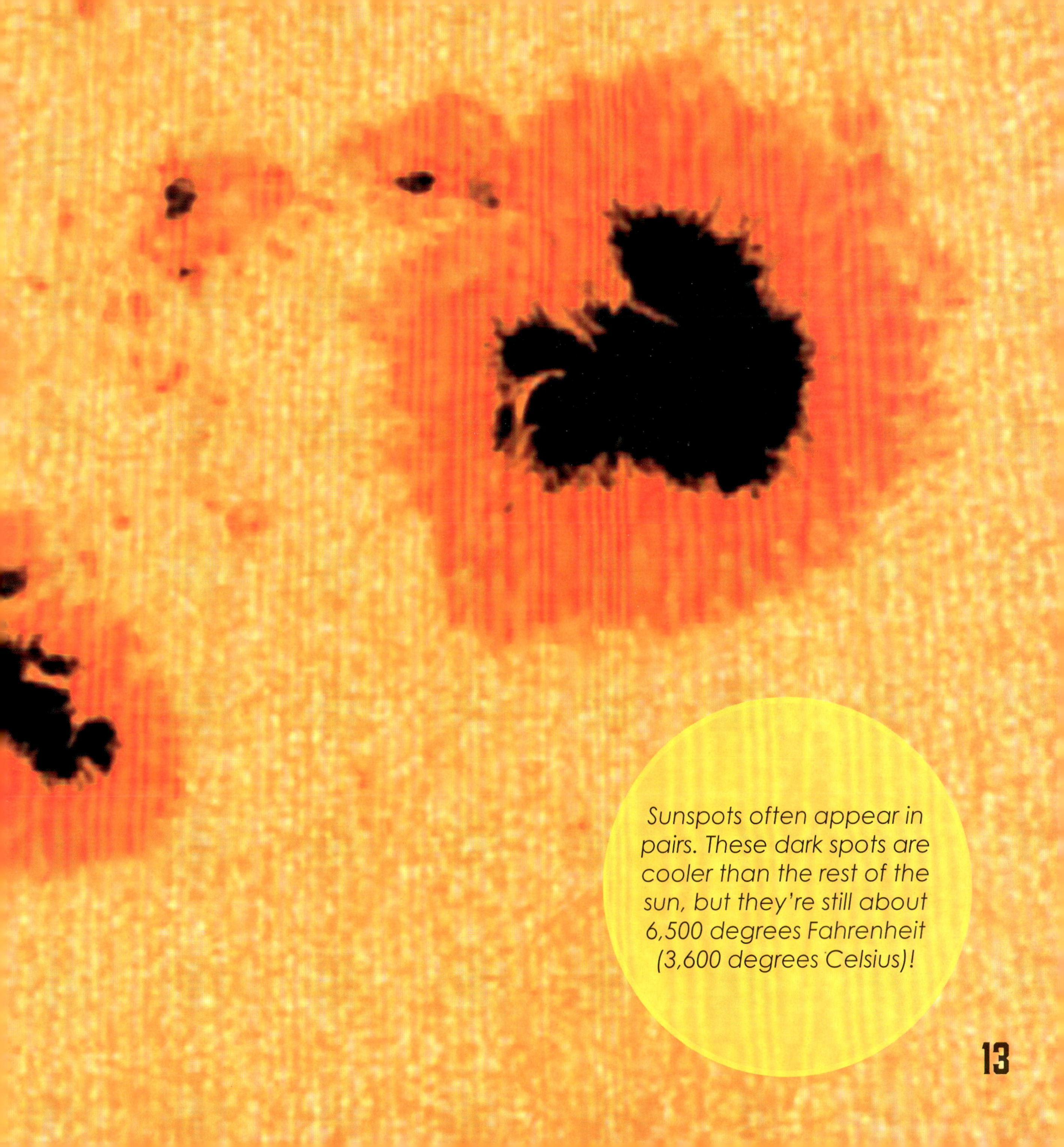

Sunspots often appear in pairs. These dark spots are cooler than the rest of the sun, but they're still about 6,500 degrees Fahrenheit (3,600 degrees Celsius)!

SEVEN LAYERS OF THE SUN

The sun has seven layers. The inner layers are the core, the **radiative** zone, and the convective zone. The outer layers are the photosphere, the chromosphere, the transition region, and the corona.

The core is the center of the sun and is the hottest part. The core also produces all the sun's energy. It takes hundreds of thousands of years for the energy from the core to reach the surface of the sun!

The next layer is called the radiative zone. This carries energy out from the core to the convective zone. Convection happens in the convective zone, where hot gas rises and cooler gas sinks. This movement helps carry energy toward the surface.

THAT'S EXTREME!

The core is about 25 percent of the entire sun. It is very dense, but it isn't solid. It's made up of ***plasma****.*

Energy can take thousands of years to travel through the radiative zone. That means the light reaching you right now was created inside the sun a very long time ago!

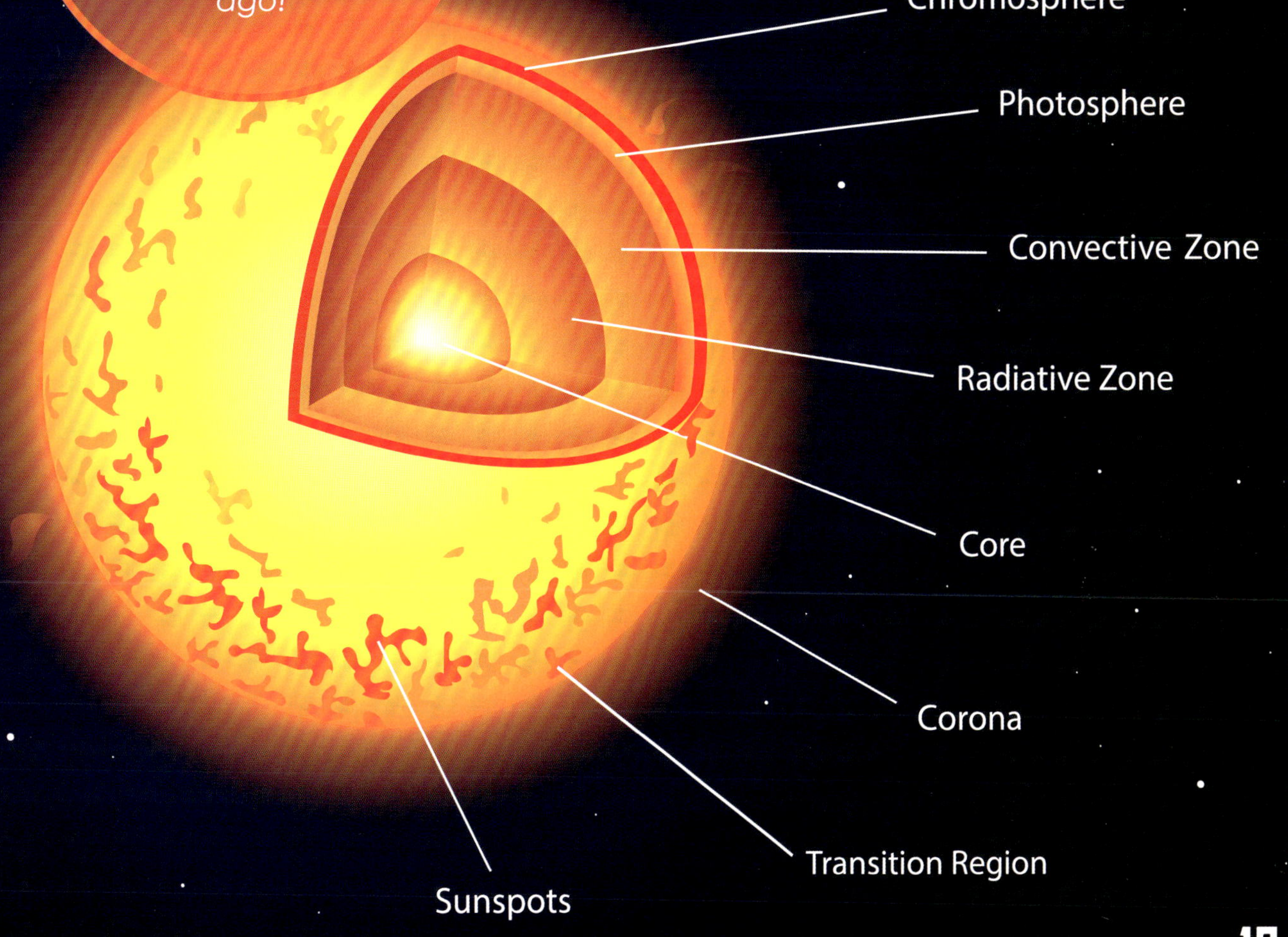

Have you ever noticed an attic is often hot, while basements stay cool? This is because warm air rises while cool air falls. The same thing happens in the sun's convective zone!

THE OUTER LAYERS

Next comes the atmosphere of the sun, starting with the photosphere. This is where the light we see from the sun comes from. The fifth layer is the chromosphere, which contains hydrogen. This gas gives off a reddish color during **eclipses**. The transition region separates the chromosphere from the corona.

The outermost layer of the sun is the corona, which is a cloud of gas and plasma. The corona extends millions of miles (km) into outer space. It gets thinner and thinner as it moves outward. The solar wind, which comes from the corona, travels all the way to Earth!

THAT'S EXTREME!

A solar eclipse happens when the moon passes between the sun and Earth. Only the sun's chromosphere and corona are visible. Special eye protection must be worn to see this safely.

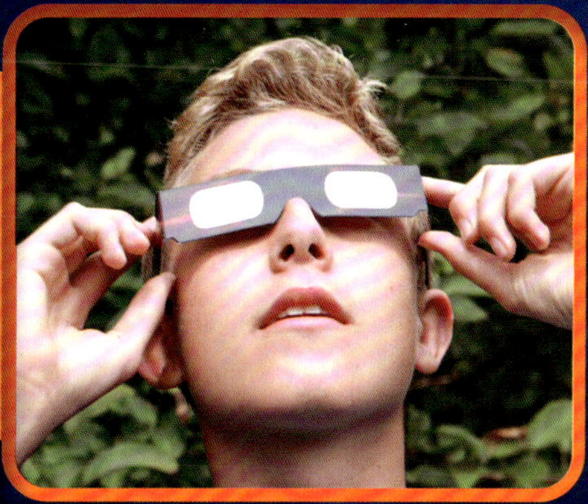

SUN AND WIND

Speaking of the solar wind, it's hot on the sun, but it's a bit breezy too! The sun's corona gets so hot that tiny bits of charged particles shoot out into space in all directions. These charged particles form a stream called the solar wind. Solar wind forms because the corona is so hot that particles escape the sun's gravity!

The solar wind from the sun also mixes with other stars' wind. These winds never stop, and they move very fast. Sometimes the solar wind even helps make colorful auroras in the sky.

THAT'S EXTREME!

Solar wind is made up of charged particles called protons and neutrons. These particles move very fast because of the sun's energy.

The atoms released from the sun travel right through our bodies without us even knowing!

THE NORTHERN LIGHTS

The solar wind can sometimes be seen on Earth as what we call the northern and the southern lights. People in some parts of the world can look into the sky and see a beautiful light show!

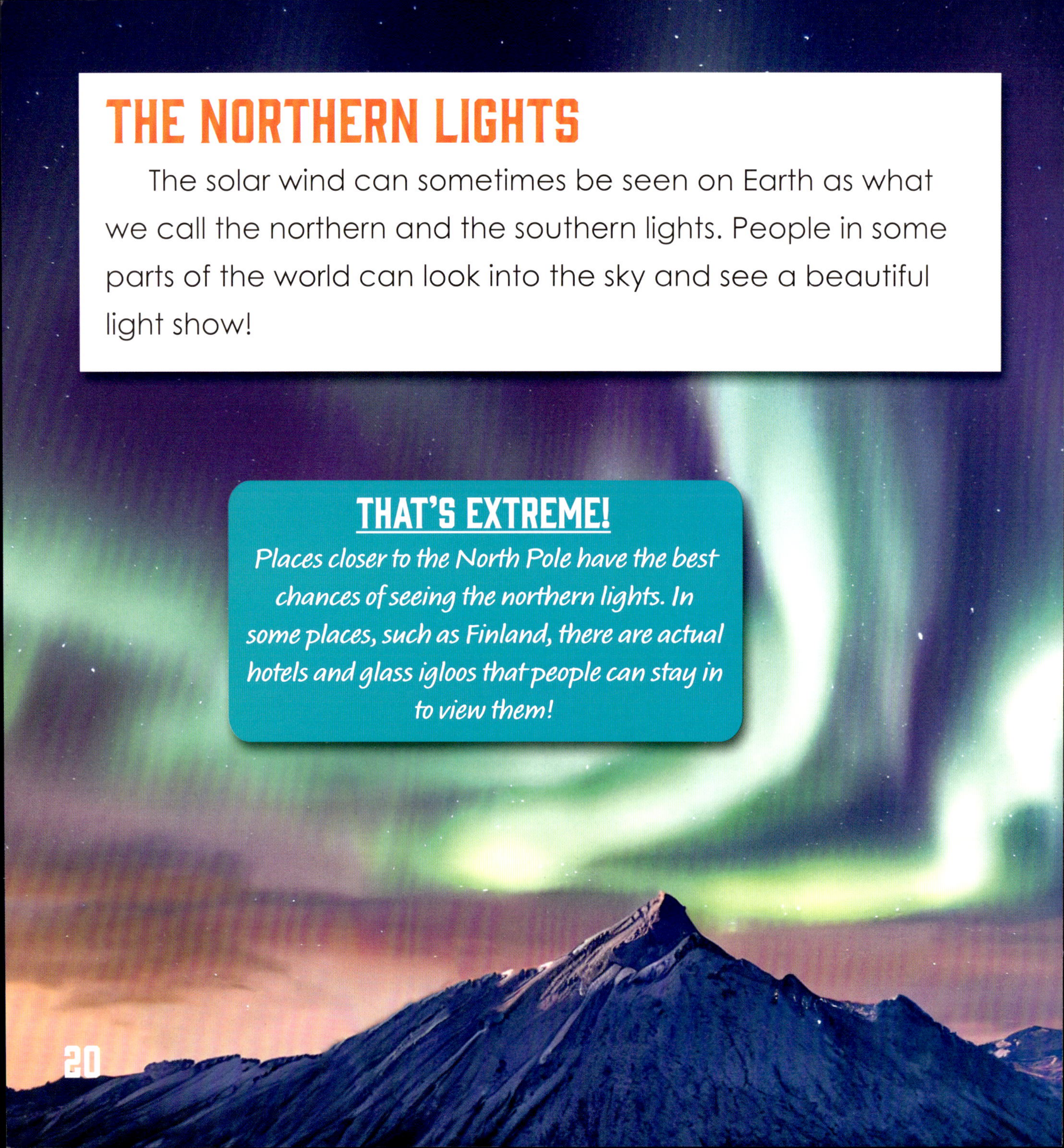

THAT'S EXTREME!

Places closer to the North Pole have the best chances of seeing the northern lights. In some places, such as Finland, there are actual hotels and glass igloos that people can stay in to view them!

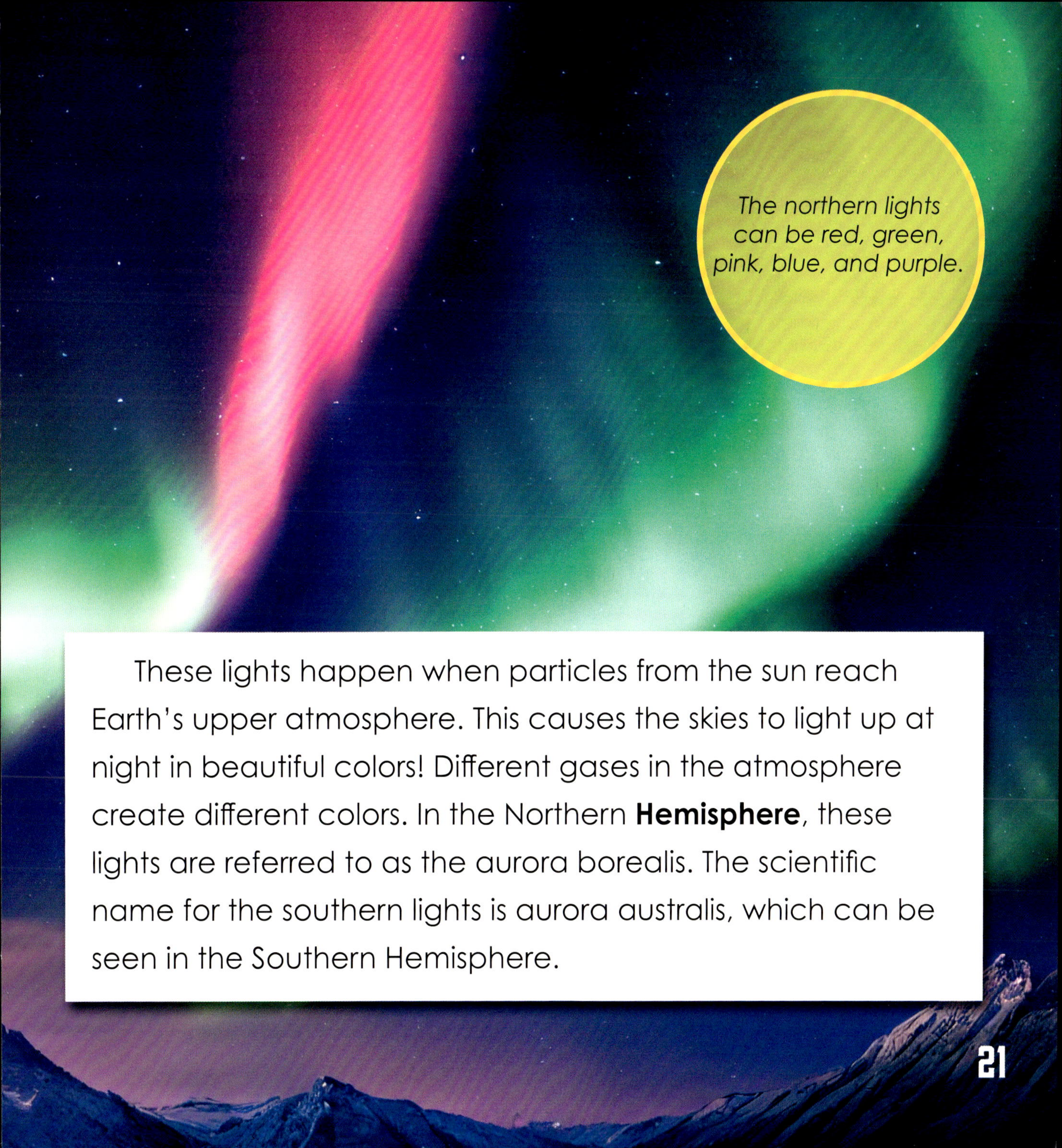

The northern lights can be red, green, pink, blue, and purple.

These lights happen when particles from the sun reach Earth's upper atmosphere. This causes the skies to light up at night in beautiful colors! Different gases in the atmosphere create different colors. In the Northern **Hemisphere**, these lights are referred to as the aurora borealis. The scientific name for the southern lights is aurora australis, which can be seen in the Southern Hemisphere.

THE SOLAR SYSTEM

Everything in the solar system orbits the sun because of its gravitational pull.

The sun contains 99.86 percent of the solar system's mass. The sun is the only object in the solar system that makes its own light. Everything else reflects, or throws back, the sun's light. Planets are colder the farther away they are from the sun. The sun's energy gets weaker with distance, so the planets that are further away receive less sunlight and heat. Mercury is the closest to the sun—and the hottest!

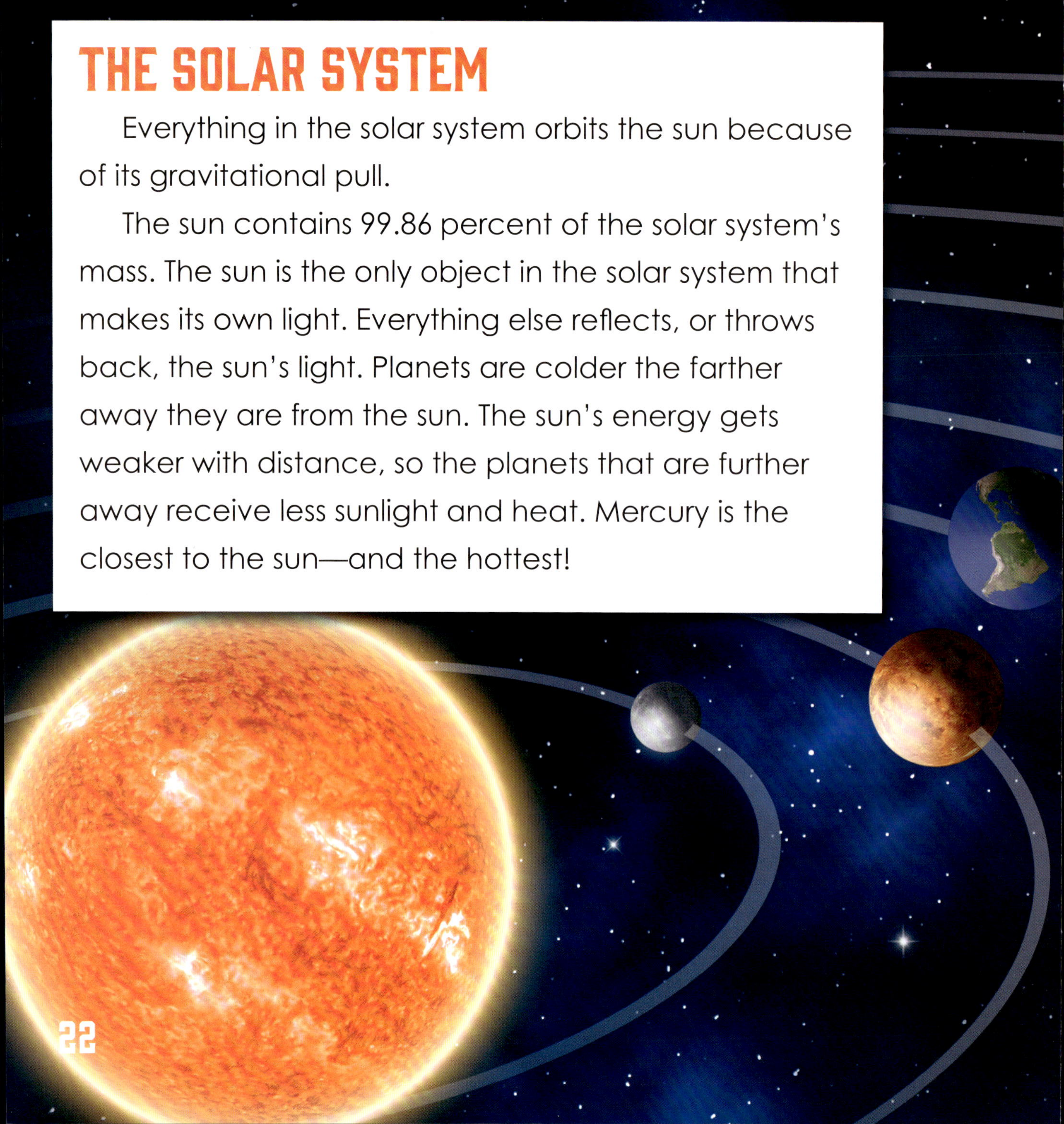

There are eight planets in our solar system.

THAT'S EXTREME!

Pluto used to be a planet, but was **reclassified** as a dwarf planet in 2006. There are four other dwarf planets in our solar system: Eris, Haumea, Makemake, and Ceres.

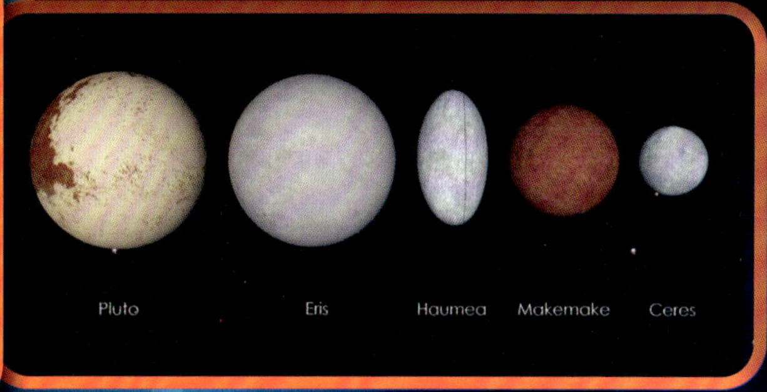

The sun also has a huge impact on Earth's oceans. It can affect the temperature of the oceans and ocean currents.

THE WEATHER

The energy from the sun helps create our weather on Earth. Since Earth is almost round and continually spinning, the sun's rays reach different parts of it at different times and angles. Temperatures are usually warmer near the **equator** because it gets more direct sun. Temperatures are milder away from the equator. They get very cold near the poles.

Earth's tilt causes seasonal changes: winter, spring, summer, and fall. The side of the Earth that's tilted toward the sun experiences warmer summer weather. The side of the Earth that's tilted away from the sun gets colder winter weather.

THAT'S EXTREME!

Even the wind on Earth is caused by the sun! Air warmed by the sun rises, and cool air moves in below it.

RUNNING OUT OF FUEL

The sun uses hydrogen for fuel. What happens if the sun runs out of hydrogen?

When stars run out of fuel, they start to change! Yellow dwarf stars start to get bigger. Then, they grow even larger and become red giant stars.

Red giant stars send out about 1,000 times more energy than our sun does. A red giant star would bake Earth. It might even blow away our atmosphere. Thankfully, scientists say the sun has about 5 billion years of hydrogen fuel left. The sun is only about halfway through its lifecycle.

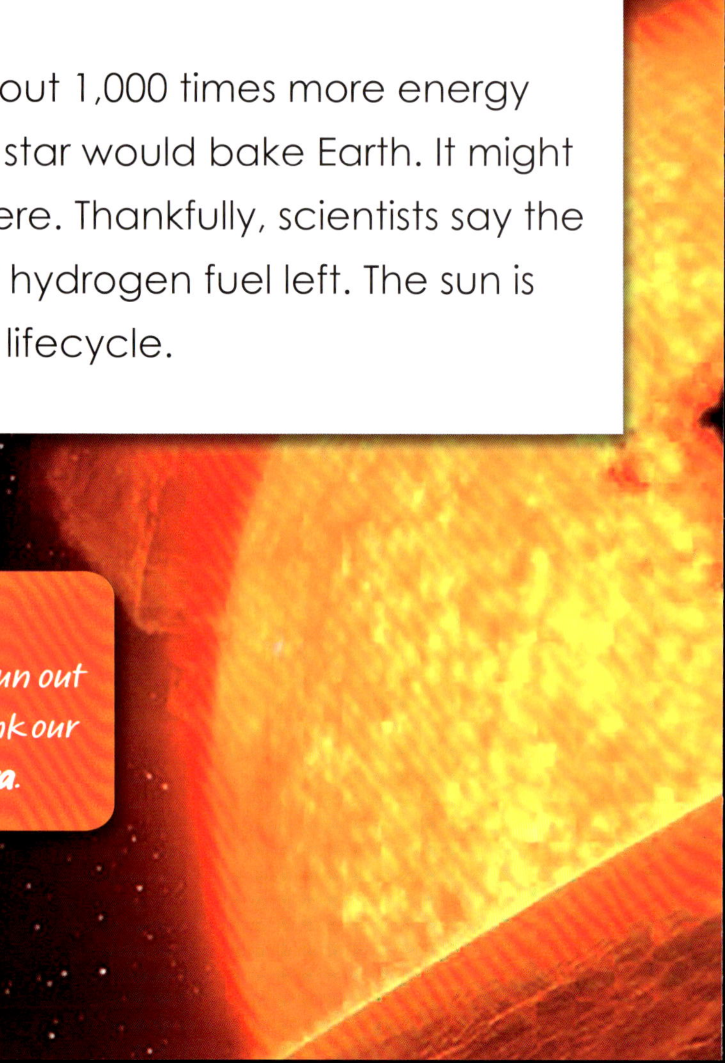

THAT'S EXTREME!

Supermassive stars explode when they run out of hydrogen fuel, but scientists don't think our sun will create that kind of ***supernova****.*

One day, our sun will grow into a red giant star. But not anytime soon!

Soak up those rays—but don't forget your sunscreen!

THE LIFE-GIVING SUN

The sun is made of about 92 percent hydrogen and 8 percent helium. The sun's gases are always moving, both inside and out! This constant motion helps create sunspots, **solar flares**, and the solar wind.

Even without a trip to space, people throughout history have understood how important the sun is to life on Earth. Without the light and energy from the sun, all life on Earth would perish. So, the next time you look up in the sky, remember how important that big yellow ball is!

THAT'S EXTREME!

No spacecrafts have visited the sun. Nothing that currently exists could handle the heat! In 2024, NASA's Parker Solar Probe got closer than anything ever had before—but it was still 3.8 million miles (5.9 million km) away!

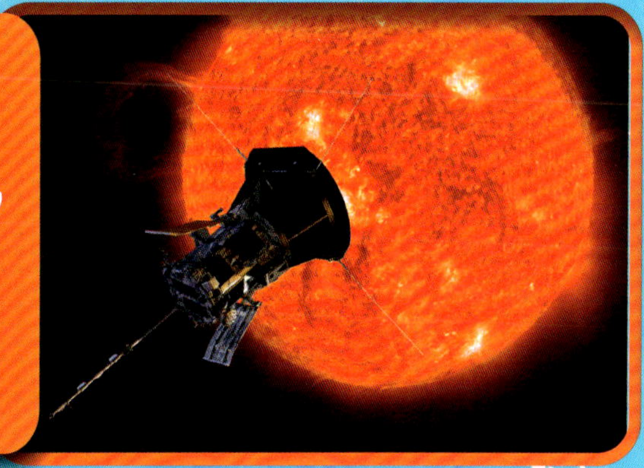

GLOSSARY

astronomer: a person who studies stars and planets

circumference: the distance around a ball-shaped object at its widest point

eclipse: when one object in space blocks another from view

equator: an imaginary line around Earth the same distance from the North and South Poles

gravity: the force that pulls objects toward the center of a planet or star

hemisphere: one half of Earth

ignite: to catch fire

orbit: travels in a circle around

plasma: a hot gas made up of parts of atoms that carry an electric charge

radiative: having to do with the process of sending out

reclassify: to put something in a new class or category

solar flare: a sudden and intense release of energy in the sun's atmosphere

supernova: the explosion of a very large star

MORE INFORMATION

BOOKS

McAnulty, Stacy. *Sun! One in a Billion.* New York, NY: Henry Holt and Co., 2018.

Seluk, Nick. *The Sun Is Kind of a Big Deal.* Albany, NY: Orchard Books, 2018.

Statum, Hilary. *Solar System for Kids.* New York, NY: Callisto Kids, 2025.

WEBSITES

Planets for Kids: Sun
planetsforkids.org/star-sun.html
Find fun facts and more about our solar system's sun here.

Sun Facts for Kids
sciencekids.co.nz/sciencefacts/space/sun.html
Learn more great facts about our sun.

Publisher's note to educators and parents: Our editors have carefully reviewed these websites to ensure that they are suitable for students. Many websites change frequently, however, and we cannot guarantee that a site's future contents will continue to meet our high standards of quality and educational value. Be advised that students should be closely supervised whenever they access the internet.

INDEX